CORNSTALKS
AND
CANNONBALLS

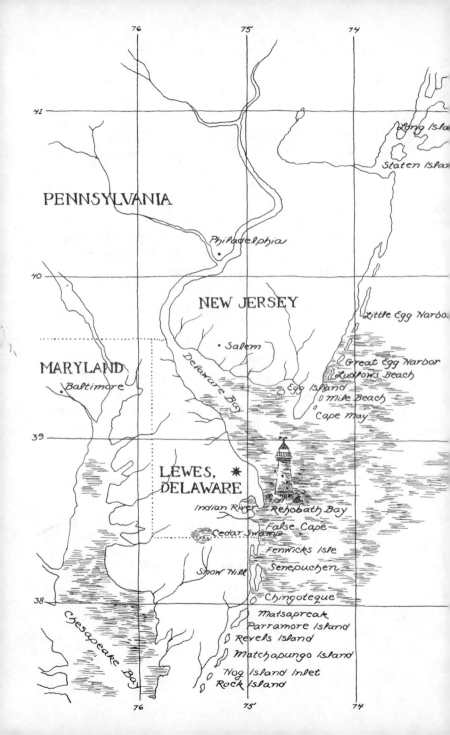

CORNSTALKS
AND
CANNONBALLS

by BARBARA MITCHELL
pictures by KAREN RITZ

PB
MIT

A YOUNG YEARLING BOOK

72

Published by
Dell Publishing
a division of
Bantam Doubleday Dell Publishing Group, Inc.
666 Fifth Avenue
New York, New York 10103

For Dr. Jordan
 —*BARBARA MITCHELL*

For my dad, the ship builder
 —*KAREN RITZ*

The trademark Yearling® is registered in the U.S. Patent and
Trademark Office.

The trademark Dell® is registered in the U.S. Patent and Trademark Office.

ISBN: 0-440-40533-5

Reprinted by arrangement with Carolrhoda Books, Inc.

Printed in the United States of America

November 1991

10   9   8   7   6   5   4   3   2

WES

A Note from the Author

This is the story of a little town in a little state. The name of the state is Delaware. The name of the town is Lewes (LOO-iss). The people of Lewes like to tell how their town fooled the English navy during the War of 1812. They have been telling the story for almost 200 years now.

Stories handed down like this are called legends. Each time a legend is told, it seems to get bigger and better. Like most legends, this one is part history and part just-for-fun. For example, the rhymes about the hen and pig come from an old book called Scharf's *History of Delaware*. They are a funny way of saying no one was hurt.

I hope you have fun reading *Cornstalks and Cannonballs*. Maybe some day you will come see this brave little town for yourself. The people of Lewes would be happy to show you the old cannons and the hole in Caleb Rodney's door.

Long ago there was a little town
by the sea.
It was called Lewes.

Lewes was a pretty town.

Sand dunes sparkled in the sun.

Fishing boats filled the bay.

At night a lighthouse glowed.

Sea birds flew.

Sea winds blew.

Lewes was a busy town.

Ship builders hammered and sawed.

They made new ships.

They fixed old ones.

Fishermen got up before the sun
to go fishing.

Farmers worked hard in their fields.

Women cooked and sewed and cleaned.
Little children played on Old Frog Hill.
Bigger children went swimming
in Sunday Monday Pond.

Grandfathers on Market Street
told stories of times gone by.
Grandmothers on Knitting Street
knit caps for their fishermen.
And all the people were very proud
of their little town.

Summer turned to fall.

Fall turned to winter.

One December day

the fishermen came home early.

They had bad news.

English ships were in the bay.

England and America were at war!

The bad news went up Market Street.

It went down Knitting Street.

"English in the bay!

What will they do?"

The English would not let
any other ships into the bay.
They would not let any boats out either.
The fishermen could not work.
All day they sat in Caleb Rodney's Store.
They talked and worried and wondered.

The first snow fell.

But mothers would not let

their little children sled

down Old Frog Hill.

Bigger children stopped skating

on Sunday Monday Pond.

Everyone watched and waited.

Weeks passed.   Then months.

The ships were full of cannons.

They were full of hungry sailors too.

"Sir John," they told their captain,

"we want meat!

We want vegetables!

We are hungry!"

They kept it up and kept it up.

So Sir John sat down and wrote a note.

> *To the people of Lewes—*
>
> *Send us meat.*
>
> *Send us vegetables.*
>
> *Or we will destroy your town.*

Sir John was sure

the little town would be afraid.

"Tomorrow we will be eating roast beef,"

he told his sailors.

"And hot potatoes. And carrots too."

But the people of Lewes were not afraid.

They were angry.

"Send you our meat and vegetables?"

they said.

"Never! You are our enemy.

We will never feed you!"

Sir John could not believe it!

He sat on his ship.

He wondered what to do next.

But the people of Lewes
did not sit still.
"Sir John will not destroy our town!"
they said.
"We will fight,"
said the farmers and the fishermen.
"Sam Davis is brave.
He will be our captain."

"Stop the hammering!
Stop the sawing!
Get busy making gunshot!"
said the ship builders.
"Get out the stew pots!
Get out the bean pots!
Our soldiers will need hot food,"
said the women.

"Clean up the old cannons!"
said the grandfathers.
They cleaned the sand
out of four old cannons
left over from the Revolutionary War.

The lighthouse man
turned out his light.
The little town waited in the dark.

By the end of March
Sir John's sailors were almost starving.
Smells of stew and beans
blew out to sea.
Those hungry sailors nearly went crazy!
"Where is our meat?
Where are our vegetables?" they shouted.
"We smell stew!
We smell baked beans!
We are hungry!"

So Sir John sent another note to the town.

I will give you one last chance.

Send us food right now.

Or else!

But the brave people would not do it.

Sir John was angrier than ever.

"Ready! Fire!" he shouted.

Cannonballs flew at the little town.

Boom! Boom! Boom! Boom!

The English fired fast.

Boom. . . . . Boom. . . . .

The little town fired slowly.

They did not have many cannonballs.

Boom.

They fired their last one.

The farmers looked at the fishermen.

The fishermen looked at the farmers.

Then they all looked over the beach.

It was covered with English cannonballs

"Let me see one of those balls,"

said a grandfather.

He took the ball to a cannon.

Smack! The ball went right in.

The English cannonballs

fit the town cannons!

"Call out the boys!" Sam Davis shouted.

Tall boys.   Short boys.

Thin boys.   Fat boys.

They all came running.

Back and forth they ran,

carrying cannonballs to the cannons.

Boom! Boom! Boom! Boom!
The English cannonballs
flew back at their own ships.
But Sam Davis was still worried.
He knew his little town
was not as strong as the English navy.
He looked at the empty fishing boats.
He looked at the pretty little houses.
He looked at the farmers' fields.
Dry cornstalks stuck up
through patches of snow.
Suddenly he smiled.

Then he shouted to the farmers.

"Bring me those cornstalks!

Bring me your farm tools!

We are going to have a bonfire!"

"A bonfire?" said the farmers.

"This is no time for a bonfire!"

But they did as they were told.

While they were gone,
Sam Davis made a fire.
When they came back,
he took a hoe.

He held it close to the fire.
Not close enough to burn it.
Just close enough to turn it black.

"Make all the tools and cornstalks black,"
he told the men.

"We want to help too," said the women.

They dressed in men's clothes.

They brought their brooms.

Girls ran to the woods for sticks.

Night came.

"The town is out of cannonballs,"

said Sir John.

"Get out the row boats.

We will row to shore and take over."

"Look, Sir!" shouted a sailor.

An army was filling the town.

Line after line they came.

Down the streets.

Across the beaches.

Out on the docks.

It was the people of the little town.

Half of them were women dressed as men.

But in the dark

Sir John could not tell that.

They all carried guns.

Those guns were really
just cornstalks and hoes
and sticks and brooms.
But in the dark
they looked real.

"They have guns!
There must be hundreds of them!"
shouted the sailor.
"There are too many for us to handle!
Back to the ships!"
said Sir John.

So the English sailors went back
to their ships.
They sailed away.
And they never came back.

The next day

the people looked over their town.

"Not much harm done," said the fishermen.

Sam Davis wrote in his book:

  One hole in milk can.

  One hole in chimney.

  One hole in Caleb Rodney's door.

"It didn't cost much," said the farmers.

Sam Davis wrote in his book:

Cost of cannonballs—$00.00

(Gift of English navy)

"No one was hurt," said the mothers.

Sam Davis wrote:

One bundle of clothes knocked off

one washerwoman's head.

The grandmothers on Knitting Street

summed it up. They said,

"The English captain and his men

Shot a pig and killed a hen."

Sam Davis wrote:

One chicken killed.

One pig wounded—leg broken.

The fishermen went back to fishing.

The ship builders went back

to building ships.

The farmers picked up their tools.

They went back to their farms.

The sea birds flew

and the sea winds blew

in that brave little town

of long ago.